SHORT BLACKS are gems of recent Australian writing – brisk reads that quicken the pulse and stimulate the mind.

SHORT BLACKS

1 Richard Flanagan *The Australian Disease: On the decline of love and the rise of non-freedom*

2 Karen Hitchcock *Fat City*

3 Noel Pearson *The War of the Worlds*

4 Helen Garner *Regions of Thick-Ribbed Ice*

5 John Birmingham *The Brave Ones: East Timor, 1999*

6 Anna Krien *Booze Territory*

7 David Malouf *The One Day*

8 Simon Leys *Prosper: A voyage at sea*

9 Robert Manne *Cypherpunk Revolutionary: On Julian Assange*

10 Les Murray *Killing the Black Dog*

11 Robyn Davidson *No Fixed Address*

12 Galarrwuy Yunupingu *Tradition, Truth and Tomorrow*

NO
FIXED
ADDRESS

ROBYN
DAVIDSON

SHORT BLACKS

Published by Black Inc.,
an imprint of Schwartz Publishing Pty Ltd
37–39 Langridge Street
Collingwood VIC 3066 Australia
enquiries@blackincbooks.com
www.blackincbooks.com

Copyright © Robyn Davidson 2006
Robyn Davidson asserts her right to be known as the author
of this work.

First published in Quarterly Essay 24, *No Fixed Address: Nomads and the
fate of the planet,* Black Inc., 2006.
This edition published 2015.

ALL RIGHTS RESERVED.
No part of this publication may be reproduced, stored in a retrieval
system, or transmitted in any form by any means electronic,
mechanical, photocopying, recording or otherwise without the prior
consent of the publishers.

National Library of Australia Cataloguing-in-Publication entry:
Davidson, Robyn, 1950– author.
No fixed address / Robyn Davidson.
9781863957731 (paperback) 9781925203578 (ebook)
Short blacks ; no.11. Nomads.
305.906918

Cover and text design by Peter Long.

Printed in Australia by Griffin Press. The paper
this book is printed on is certified against the
Forest Stewardship Council® Standards. Griffin
Press holds FSC chain of custody certification
SGS-COC-005088. FSC promotes environmentally
responsible, socially beneficial and economically
viable management of the world's forests.

Robyn Davidson's books include *Tracks* and *Desert Places*. She edited the *Picador Book of Journeys* and her essays have appeared in *Granta*, *The Monthly* and *National Geographic*.

INDIAN HIMALAYAS

The house sits at seven thousand feet. To the south-west, just visible through a gap in the hills which are like stacked slices of ever paler blue glass, is the Gangetic plain, under a pall of dust. To the north-east, the rampart of rock and ice that is the Himalayas proper, on the other side of which lies Tibet. To reach the house from the nearest road, one must climb through three thousand feet of Himalayan oak forest, along a rough path. One must hire ponies or men to carry all the luggage and provisions up to the house.

I love this place and would like to be buried here.

When I say "this place", of course I don't just mean the house and its setting. I mean the people who live around me, some of whom work for me as servants, gardeners, stonemasons, porters and so on. I provide one of the very few opportunities for employment in these hills.

Most of the original oak from this area – the Kumaon – was taken out by the British during the world wars. They replaced it with introduced pine which dries out the soil and inhibits the seeding of native species. The four hundred acres on which I live is re-growth native oak, and one of the few patches of it in the Kumaon region. Every time I drive from the railhead to the village below, on my way back here from Australia or London, I notice another hillside thinned of timber, another patch of forest uprooted to make a tiny terraced field, another landslide on these geologically new, precipitous inclines.

The peasants are wholly aware that they are responsible for their forest disappearing, for their water disappearing, but they have no choice. If they do not chop wood, how will they cook and stay warm? If they do not carve out new fields from the forest, what will their sons do? As it is, many have to go to towns and cities to find work. If they do not have several children, who will take care of them when they are old, or provide the labour needed when the crops are ready? Many children die, after all. If they do not lop the trees for feed for their animals, or allow them to graze in the forest, the animals will starve. If they do not snare the leopards, or poison them, the leopards will take their animals or, worse still, their children. With the loss of forest goes the loss of game, and that makes for hungry leopards. There is no safety net for the peasants here. One stroke of bad luck, and total, irremediable ruin is their fate. Here, poverty is the cause of ecological catastrophe, not ignorance, not greed.

The farms are small, hand-made terraces radiating down cleared hillsides. Three or four crops are grown in a year – wheat, corn, potatoes, cabbage, peas. The work is backbreaking, the yield, subsistence. The weather is harsh – freezing winters, hail in spring, dry early summers, a late summer monsoon which washes soil down into the river far below. Ploughing is done with oxen. Monkeys, pigs, bears and deer take their portion of crop yields. With the clearing of oak, whose roots hold water in the catchment slopes, springs dry up. Domestic animals are taken out for grazing in the national forests and eat out any young oak which is highly nutritious but slow-growing. Seedlings don't stand a chance against desiccation and over-grazing. Women range all day through the remaining forest, cutting wood for cooking fires, or gathering huge bundles of grass for their animals, which they carry home on their heads. They work unbelievably hard, but are in poor health, due to poor nutrition.

The diet is principally wheat flour, lentils, sugar, milk, a few vegetables and spice. Nevertheless they tend to have many pregnancies, despite the government's advertising campaign promoting two children only. That policy has nothing to do with the exigencies of their lives.

There are fights within families over land. Sons who cannot inherit have to find other farmland or work elsewhere. There is little arable land left, and that is prohibitively expensive. (A lot of it now is being bought up by developers, catering to the wealthy middle class who want to return to bucolic simplicity during their holidays, who build large cement houses containing all the mod cons, and clear any trees that spoil the view.) Dispossessed peasants must join the drain of rural people heading to the city. Usually they will live in poverty and squalor there, scraping enough to get by in menial jobs, or begging in the streets. Sometimes, if they have managed to sell land, they set up small businesses and join the burgeoning middle class on its bottom rung. Either way, life is precarious.

If there is a particularly bad year or two, so that the farms fall below subsistence, then most of the men will have to leave to find other work. Women must still go out almost all day to gather wood. Children are looked after by old people. Or they look after themselves. Children and old people must do all the farm labour. And that labour is great because it is a perpetual wrestling with the forest – keeping it back, digging it up, building fences against it, changing it, trying to stave off its fecund complexity for growth that is uniform and predictable. It's an all-day, all-night job, year in, year out, defying nature's processes. The peasants here are wary of change. It takes them a long time to try something new, to do things another way. They are not flexible people. There is no leeway for mistakes.

I am witnessing archaic agriculture at first hand – the aftershocks of the most important revolution the human race has ever undergone.

I have managed to keep my four hundred acres of re-growth oak in tact. No wood-cutting is allowed here; no farm animals graze in the forest. The women are invited to cut grass once a year, but they cannot lop and destroy the trees. At first they considered me an impediment to be got around. But when water began to flow back into their springs, the policy was accepted. Wildlife has begun to return to the area.

I like my neighbours very much. And I depend on them just as they depend on me. I would like to do something for them, apart from offering employment. I would like to set up a local industry in which they can participate. Tourism, for example. The stressed and alienated of the First World can come and enjoy the simplicity, sweetness and grace of the Third. If there is more money to be made in accommodating and serving such visitors than in farming, then the remaining forest can be preserved. And from a more secure economic base improvements in the peasant's quality of life can be generated. Those benefits of modern civilisation such as effective medicine and literacy. The easing of daily anxiety, of internecine squabbling and land grabbing, of grinding, bone-cracking labour. Everyone will benefit.

Well, perhaps not everyone. Not in the long term, anyway. Not in relation to the Big Picture.

My neighbours use incomparably less of the world's resources than tourists do. Than I do. I drive a car. I dash around the world in aeroplanes. I use washing machines and forget to turn off electric lights. I throw out more garbage in a week than these peasants would in a year.

As a product of the First World, I enjoy a better standard of living than ever before in history. But that is because I belong to an elite, dependent on materials imported from countries with large, impoverished populations. I live on a higher step of a pyramidal social structure that gradually formed around the settled life, and continues to be essential to the world economy. It is a myth that globalising, free-market capitalism will secure everyone a position at the top. We know perfectly well that the earth's resources simply could not cope – are already not coping. For some of us to retain the standard of living we have become used to, others of us will have to provide the cheap labour, and remain poor. I might be able to help a few peasants up onto a higher level of the pyramid, but their vacated rung will quickly be filled by others less fortunate.

The agricultural revolution led directly to the benefits people like me enjoy. But they are available to the few at the expense of the many. This is axiomatic.

> And Adam knew Eve his wife; and she conceived, and bare Cain, and said, I have gotten a man from the Lord.

And she again bare his brother Abel. And
Abel was a keeper of sheep, but Cain was a
tiller of the ground.

And in process of time it came to pass, that
Cain brought of the fruit of the ground an
offering unto the Lord.

And Abel, he also brought of the firstlings
of his flock and of the fat thereof. And
the Lord had respect unto Abel and to his
offering:

But unto Cain and to his offering he had not
respect. And Cain was very wroth, and his
countenance fell.

And the Lord said unto Cain, Why art thou
wroth? and why is thy countenance fallen?
If thou doest well, shalt thou not be
accepted? and if thou doest not well, sin
lieth at the door: and unto thee shall be his
desire, and thou shalt rule over him.

And Cain talked with Abel his brother: and
it came to pass, when they were in the field,

that Cain rose up against Abel his brother,
and slew him.

And the Lord said unto Cain, Where is
Abel thy brother? And he said, I know not:
Am I my brother's keeper?

And he said, What hast thou done? the
voice of thy brother's blood crieth unto me
from the ground.

And now art thou cursed from the earth,
which hath opened her mouth to receive thy
brother's blood from thy hand.

When thou tillest the ground, it shall not
henceforth yield unto thee her strength; a
fugitive and a vagabond shalt thou be in the
earth.

And Cain said unto the Lord, My punishment is greater than I can bear.

Behold, thou hast driven me out this day
from the face of the earth; and from thy face
shall I be hid; and I shall be a fugitive and a
vagabond in the earth; and it shall come to

> pass, that every one that findeth me shall slay me.
>
> And the Lord said unto him, Therefore whosoever slayeth Cain, vengeance shall be taken on him sevenfold. And the Lord set a mark upon Cain, lest any finding him should kill him.
>
> And Cain went out from the presence of the Lord, and dwelt in the land of Nod, on the east of Eden.
>
> And Cain knew his wife; and she conceived, and bare Enoch: and he builded a city, and called the name of the city, after the name of his son, Enoch.

I read this Genesis allegory as a brief history of prehistory, the rise of agriculture and settlement, and, eventually, the creation of cities or, as we like to call it, civilisation.

Eden is the state of animality, before language and imagination set us apart from other animals. Man is "evicted" from this state, into the pain of self-consciousness and awareness of mortality.

At a point in the story, there is a divergence. Cain plants crops and remains in one place. Abel continues to wander, either as a hunter-gatherer or as a herdsman-hunter.

Cain's agricultural produce is inferior to Abel's. It is high-calorie, low-protein, homogeneous bulk. The starchy grain can feed more people but at a lower standard of nutrition. Cain's workers have much less leisure time than their nomadic cousins who are not only healthier, they are not afflicted by periodic famine. In hard times they can move elsewhere to find food.

Compared to Abel of the wilderness, Cain and his people are short, overworked and full of parasites. Their teeth are rotten. Their mortality rate is high. Their bones are rickety, and they suffer from the infectious diseases and epidemics that cannot exist among people who shift around all the time. Women of Cain have lost much of their autonomy. They have far more pregnancies than women of Abel, because farmers need lots of children as a labour force.

There are, therefore, many more Cains than Abels. And even though they are wormy and stunted and malnourished, their unprecedented numbers can defeat, or simply subsume, small bands of nomads.

Cain is no longer his "brother's keeper" in the sense that individual possession of stored food takes the place of the food-sharing habits of nomads. Hunter-gatherers don't produce surplus, and they can't carry much weight. Therefore there is virtually no social ranking or dominance of the kind needed to hoard, redistribute, steal or protect excess food. Abel's people are essentially egalitarian (as modern nomads still are). Men and women together contribute to the survival of the group, with women often providing the majority of calories.

Cain continues to plant crops on land that begins to lose its fertility. Or he's faced with a drought, or eroding flood, or the land is divided up among too many descendants so there's no longer enough of it for subsistence. Descendants who cannot inherit have to go elsewhere, as "vagabonds, fugitives", to find new land to cultivate. Wherever they go in country given over to agriculture, they are threatened and turned away. There is no room for them and they must resort to reclaiming land from the "jungle". There they must drive off, incorporate or kill competing nomads.

Self-sufficient villages form. The house becomes the centre of an entirely new social organisation and locus of production. Women's range of activity shrinks further. The new code of domestic morality is about the safeguarding of property, and that includes her. Her protection is also captivity. People have to find new ways to organise private and public space, new ways to describe time, new ways to socialise, new ways to cope with friction and with violence. Alcohol enters the scene. Cain is the first drunk.

Greater food surpluses lead to more complex settlements requiring specialists – full-time craftsmen, priests and chiefs. A nascent elite controls the resources of increasing numbers of people. Society, already stratified by the altered requirements of agriculture, begins to segregate and separate further, into classes and castes. Rulers grow in power, reinforcing their authority through warrior castes whose role is to accrue and protect wealth. Different professions acquire different ranks. Social opportunity declines as boundaries harden between groups.

Walls are now necessary, because surplus food stored behind them attracts raiders. There were war-like skirmishes in Abel's world too, of course. But now, for the first time, there is surplus worth stealing, making warfare chronic.

When these societies coalesce into cities, part two of the agricultural revolution begins. The urban revolution. It is characterised by high-density living, hierarchy, bureaucracy, regimentation and a ruling class in command of a farming underclass. The social pyramid necessary for intensified agricultural production to feed the city is locked into place, including the coercive institutions needed to hold it all together – armies, tax collectors, police, religious institutions. Warfare develops beyond raiding to conquest and subjugation. It is aggrandised into an "heroic" calling. In a habitat already filled, the losers cannot just go away and form a new community. There is now nowhere to go. Defeated groups are either killed or enslaved.

Abel's people are driven almost to extinction. The old habitats, once rich in game and wild foods, have been transformed and can no longer sustain them. All that is left to them is land that farmers cannot use – deserts, frozen tundra, high-altitude pastures. Everywhere else, the domestic has replaced the wild, and the change is irreversible.

The new economic mode is not without advantages. Specialised groups of artists and artisans can produce "great" architecture, and the "great" art adorning it. But it belongs to the Nobles and the Priests. The tallying necessary for bureaucrats measuring and trading grain evolves into writing which stores cultural information. But it is only accessible to the educated elite. Goods, power and information thus condense at the top of the pyramid. In nomadic societies, the entire culture is encapsulated in each individual.

Cain's people have traded immersion in nature for domination of it. In order to eat, they have to keep nature at bay, hacking back jungle growth, uprooting weeds, changing water systems for irrigation, clearing forest for new fields. Nature becomes an opponent, something subservient to human will. They have changed from *Homo sapiens sapiens* to *Homo arrogans*.

Hobbes's vision of humanity's dystopia before the invention of the plough – "No arts; no letters; no society; and which is worst of all, continual fear and danger of violent death; and the life of man, solitary, poor, nasty, brutish, and short" – would better describe the life of a penniless ex-peasant, living away from his family in a city, than it would, say, that of a traditional Aboriginal. The streets of Delhi and Bombay are filled with such souls:

> His poor self,
> A dedicated beggar to the air,
> With his disease of all-shunned poverty,
> Walks, like contempt, alone.
> – WILLIAM SHAKESPEARE, *Timon of Athens*

STANLEY PARK

The Western Queensland cattle station where I was born was rather small by outback standards. It was dry country, just beyond the Darling Downs, but not the kind of desert that demands a few million acres to run a profit on livestock.

Our land was relatively untouched – had been minimally cleared, and never ploughed. Leichhardt passed across it on one of his expeditions inland, leaving an L-marked tree up in our brigalow forest. A dry white-sand river-bed, lined by eucalyptus, snaked along a hundred metres from the house – a simple, weatherboard building on stilts, flanked by rainwater tanks that had been empty for years, and gauzed verandahs. A windmill clanked all day. There was a tin shed for storing hay and saddlery for the stock horses. My father ran Hereford cattle, and never overstocked. By the time I came along, he was wealthy enough to buy a ute. Before that the only transport was horse and cart.

He was a very knowledgeable naturalist and geologist, and he loved the bush with a passion. He'd walked around East Africa for many years, between the wars, alternately harpooning crocodiles and prospecting for gold. He was a man's man, Edwardian in spirit, empirical as an Englishman, but a bit of a dreamer. He was happiest when he was alone out bush, boiling a billy and watching nature perform around him. There were many deadly snakes in that area, but they didn't worry him at all. If they were in or near the house, he'd catch them behind the head, let them coil around his arm, then take them down to the river-bed and let them go. He taught me basic astronomy and geology before I was six, and it was from him I absorbed my love of the natural world, and confidence within it.

He was from a long line of Queensland squattocracy – grazier pioneers whose legacy was a sense of upper-class entitlement. They were marked by eccentricity and haughtiness, a dislike of the pettiness and restrictions of the middle class, yet a direct and usually affectionate relationship with their workers. They talked about the blacks as being "bush aristocrats" or "poor old Abos". When Aborigines were taken off the stations to be sent to Mission Reserves, my forebears were dead against it, believing the blacks would be better off staying on their country. There are photographs of "the blacks' camp", women dressed in long skirts and high-necked Victorian blouses, men in stockman's gear, humpies made of mulga and tin.

Even as a child (and all the indigenous people had long gone by then), I felt that Stanley Park was missing something. And whatever that something was gave the land a mournful quality. All that blinding, drenching light, yet you got the sense there was darkness in it. Like the backing on a mirror.

The only information I had about "poor old Abos" was from my father saying how sad it was that they had to die out. Survival of the fittest made this inevitable. I pored over a book called *Customs of the World*, published in the '20s, which showed photographs of naked men wearing tall head-dresses of feathers and paint. I held in my hand the stone axes, spears and the pointing bone that my father had collected, or been given, and thought about the other hands that had held them, during those incomprehensibly long reaches of previous time.

My father loved natural bushland, but this did not prevent him from "improving" it. He would go out on his horse before dawn, up to the escarpment brigalow, to ringbark those tough little trees with his axe. No doubt he could see, even then, that once the brigalow was gone, erosion followed quickly enough in that barren white soil. But the impenetrable brigalow made mustering difficult, so it had to go.

My father sold up after a seven-year drought had drained his bank account dry. The drought was broken by a fantastic storm, and I remember a foot of hail around the house – my first encounter with ice. Then the river came down – swirling mud-coloured torrents carrying torn-up trees, breaking its banks and threatening to take our house with it. There was no capital left with which to shore up the river-bank against the next floods. So we sold Stanley Park to a gentleman farmer with pots of money, and moved east.

In all the time that whitefellas had lived among blackfellas, it had not occurred to the former that they might have a great deal to learn from the latter. That was a thought it was impossible to have, because Aborigines were the children of the race of man, and you don't take children's reasoning seriously.

Such are the forms of delusion that can occur when systems of belief obscure the obvious.

Christian missionaries and government worked together to save the souls of the blacks, and the first step towards conversion was to instill a Protestant, agriculture-based work ethic. Flierl, a Lutheran missionary in North Queensland, stated, for example, that "The Aboriginals are nomads. Nothing can be done among them without settling them down on reserves. They are not used to hard work, and very slow in leaving their former manners and customs..."

His successor, Pfalzer, extended that view with: "The only thing that could keep these widely roaming hordes together at all is work. But if they are to work they must be fed. And we will not have the necessary food for them unless we cultivate the land."

Ritual maintenance of sacred sites was prevented, sundering people from their country, which is to say, from meaning and identity. Trauma after trauma was inflicted, sometimes viciously, sometimes with indifference, and sometimes with good intentions.

So it must have been, in some form or another, along the interface between settlement and nomadism, for ten thousand years.

The ideology ingrained in my father was Social Darwinism. It allowed him to believe that it was regrettable, even tragic, but ultimately unavoidable that a race and all its achievements should disappear, that the people who had worked for your family and helped them build up their cattle stations could be evicted from their own land and shunted off somewhere, never to be seen again. The words "concentration camp" had not entered the vernacular, and Robespierre's dictum that you had to break eggs to make omelettes had not yet been ironised. Faith in limitless progress fostered the belief that the beloved bush could be carved up into small parcels, emptied of wildlife that competed with stock, radically transformed and turned to the production of wealth, without any unpleasant kickback.

When I think back to Stanley Park now, I see it as a palimpsest of two modes of thinking. There was nomadic thinking: nomads range over country, allowing foraged areas to recuperate. Their survival is secured principally through observing and working with their environment, rather than battling against it. Then there was the kind of thinking that arose when humans became sedentary and began to conceive of land as something that could be possessed, dominated, *transformed*. It was the beginning of a detached perspective: its emblem, the fence.

In Aboriginal society a boundary or border is not a fixed line of division so much as a fuzzy set of relationships – interchanges of rights and duties, like pathways – across shared territory. Flexibly bounded places, or Countries, might be occupied by different cultural groups, speaking different languages, and sometimes antagonistic to each other, but nevertheless linked at a higher conceptual level by the net-like structure of the Dreaming – the original "theory of everything".

Scholars are still trying to describe the "Dreaming" in such a way as to make it accessible to non-Aboriginal understanding. Firstly, the word itself is something of a linguistic cock-up by an anthropologist attempting to translate an Arrernte word "Altyerre" – the meaning of which is largely unrelated to the English notion of dreams. T.G.H. Strehlow thought that a better translation would be "Eternal, Uncreated".

Difficulties arise not just because of the immense complexity of traditional Aboriginal world-views (which are also changing in response to immigrant ideas), but because of differences in the very foundations of descriptions of reality. We all believe our world constructs must be universal. The Western mind assumes that a linear time progression – marked off along its infinite stretch by remote, recent, present, soon, far-off – is the natural, even innate, orientation. It is difficult to imagine a consciousness in which that way of thinking is all but absent, in which history is absorbed into changelessness, and events (temporality) are turned into places.

No matter how much I read about the Dreaming, the confidence that I understand it never quite takes root in my mind. To me it is on a par with, say, quantum mechanics, or string theory – ideas you think you grasp until you have to explain them. Each time I attempt it, I have to feel my way into it again, and I am never sure of my ground.

One could say that the Dreaming is a spiritual realm which saturates the visible world with meaning; that it is the matrix of being; that it was the time of creation; that it is a parallel universe which may be contacted via the ritual performance of song, dance and painting; that it is a network of stories of mythological heroes – the forerunners and creators of contemporary man.

During the creation period, the ancestral beings made journeys and performed deeds: they fought, loved, hunted, behaved badly or well, rather like the Greek gods, and where they camped or hurled spears or gave birth, tell-tale marks were left in the earth. While creating this topography, they were morphing constantly from animal to human and back to animal, again rather like the Greeks.

They made separate countries, but interlaced them (related them) with their story tracks. They created frameworks for kin relations. Many different ancestors created a country, by travelling across it and meeting each other. In that way, a particular country is shared by all the creatures who live there, their essences arising from the

Dreaming, and returning to it. Some Dreamings crossed many countries, interacting with local ones as they went, and connecting places far from each other. Thus the pulse of life spreads, blood-like, through the body of the continent – node/pathway, node/pathway – as far as, and sometimes into, the sea.

At the end of that epoch, exhausted by their work, they sank back into the ground at sacred sites, where their power remains in a condensed form.

It's not quite right, however, to say that the creation period is in the past, because it is a past that is eternal and therefore also present. Ancestors sink back into, but also emerge from and pass through sites. In other words, an ancestor's journey, or story, became a place, and that place holds past, present and future simultaneously.

For traditionally oriented Aboriginal people, the historical past lies a couple of generations back, *and it always will.* The Dreaming encompasses and surrounds this time of living memory, which sinks into it. Time sinks into place, into Country.

Each sacred site contains a potentially limitless supply of the particular species left there by an ancestor. But in order to ensure their continued generation, ceremonial action is required. If this isn't done, or isn't done properly, that lifeform will eventually disappear. Children, too, are born from the ancestor's spirit which arises out of its place to impregnate a woman. Such children belong to and have responsibility for that place, and will return to it after death, so that its life potential isn't dissipated.

Not only did the mythical ancestors give the world its shape, they imbued it with moral and social structures – handing down laws whereby all humans have equal intrinsic value and a share of goods. Living by these laws invigorates the life-force surging and burgeoning through the land. In fact, to sing a ritual song is to move that ancestor along through the land. Earth is sacred, sentient stuff, it is not a counterpoint to heaven. Heaven and earth are embedded together, on the same plane. A country is saturated in consciousness. It recognises and responds to people. It *depends* on people. And just as people torn from their country are lost in non-meaning, country without its people is "orphaned" and in peril. When the web of the Dreaming is torn, the consequences for land and life are dire.

In other words, there is no distinction between the material and the spiritual, so ancestor, story, place, painting, ritual object, song and singer are all, in essence, the same thing. Dreaming tracks (or stories or songs) lace the whole of the continent. Australia itself is a narrative.

It's as if the creative potential of a whole culture, instead of being dissipated on the production of material wealth, has concentrated itself into the never-ending translation of all phenomena into one elegant, all-encompassing symbol. It is this astonishing intellectual feat that allowed indigenous people to inhabit this country so successfully, and for so long. Not just a knowledge of the landscape as a surface of separate things, but an engagement with the deeper processes and patterns and connections between things. Patterns, connections, pathways: these are emphasised. Agricultural world-views shift that emphasis to abstract geometry, division and separation, boundaries.

Traditionally oriented Aborigines are constantly on the move, but paradoxically they are existentially the most stationary people on earth. Like the Dreamings, they move eternally along the tracks and networks, but remain rooted in and identified with certain places. The ancestors stopped travelling and sank into sacred sites, but they are also simultaneously present at each of the many sites along their creation journey. They are eternally travelling and eternally fixed, like the human beings who created them and were created by them. People of the Dreaming are always "at home" in the deepest possible sense.

Compare that to extreme forms of the detached perspective that agriculture gave us. The Rapture fundamentalists, for example, who ecstatically await the end of the world which, they say, should be any day now. Things like global warming, wars in the Middle East, and ecological collapse are signs of the prophesied apocalypse, and they are to be encouraged because after Armageddon, Christ will take up true believers, of which there are frighteningly large numbers – several million it is said. For them heaven is our true home; earth expendable rubbish.

It is a pathology that places man so far outside nature, so alienated from the earth, that he would happily destroy it entirely. In its place, pyramid heaven, with a life-hating God on top.

I don't pretend to have entered the consciousness of a traditional Aboriginal person. But I imagine sometimes what it might feel like to have such a different perspective. Is it a nowness that spreads out into the place you are in, containing the flow of time? Rather like that trance-like state we experienced as children when everything seemed to unfold in an enormous billowing present. Or perhaps it is like a piece of music – a unity which nevertheless unfolds heterogeneously through time. It is said that when Mozart opened a musical manuscript he hadn't seen before, he "heard" the piece all at once, all in the same moment.

Aboriginal culture was always responding to change, always dynamic. But after colonisation, it had to make sense of the tidal wave of otherness overwhelming it. The Dreaming is changing rapidly in response to those challenges, but it continues to try to mend itself, in order to keep life going.

CONCLUSION

The agricultural revolution transformed the earth and changed the fate of humanity. It produced an entirely new mode of subsistence, which remains the foundation of the global economy to this day.

There is no going back. Without human labour hacking at the weeds, or redirecting water, domesticated grains would die out, and without that grain, so would we. The economy which gave us more cheap food, and an increasing population dependent on that food, provided no exit other than famine.

When *Homo sapiens sapiens* inherited the earth, we numbered perhaps a third of a million. Around ten thousand years ago, we had increased to perhaps three million, and by the time farming had given rise to civilisation five thousand years ago, there might have been up to twenty million of us in the world. We are now six billion and rising.

By requiring us to become sedentary, agriculture changed the way we conceive of our place in nature, and it changed the way we distributed goods. In pre-agricultural societies social structures were more or less egalitarian and food was shared. Population was limited. Injustice and subjugation did not begin with settlement (one only need look at Jane Goodall's work with chimps to know that murderousness is a primate inheritance), but they found a rich habitat there in which to flourish.

The process of agricultural take-over of hunter-gatherer economies has almost reached its conclusion. In 10,000 BC all human beings were hunters and gatherers; by 1500 AD this had reduced to about 1 per cent. And by the mid-twentieth century, it was down to 0.001 per cent.

What damage do we cause ourselves when the earliest extant efforts of the human mind to find its place in the universe have gone, never to be recovered?

And now the more recent forms of nomadism – pastoralism and artisanship – are also being brought to a halt. They do not fit well with modernising drives. Such nomads are difficult to control and tax, independent-minded, skeptical, and they tend to value knowledge above accumulated wealth.

Agriculture set us on a path to the urban and industrial revolutions, and finally to the wild consumerism of late capitalism. Like those previous chapters of the agricultural story, post-industrial globalisation is achieving material wealth, longer life, greater choice. But it cannot distribute those benefits. The rate at which the gap between over- and under-privileged is widening depends on which statistics you read, but no one seriously doubts that it is widening, both within and between countries. Evidence from its own institutions indicates that a couple of billion people suffer from chronic malnutrition and live in poverty.

Most importantly, the generation of that wealth requires an increasing pillage of the environment. Global warming alone should be terrifying enough to galvanise us into changing habits of consumption. It does not appear to be doing so. Four billion years of life on earth. Millions of those years reigned over by the dinosaurs. Us lot a mere 200,000-year blip and according to several commentators, including Lord Rees, the UK Astronomer Royal, we are not looking good to get through the next hundred years, let alone compete with the dinosaurs.

One of the questions we need to ask, if we're to have a future, is "Where, when, in what situations, did we cause less damage to ourselves, to our environment, and to our animal kin?" One answer is: when we were nomadic. It was when we settled that we became strangers in a strange land, and wandering took on the quality of banishment. Pilgrimage – religious or secular – remained as a relic of the hunting and foraging life.

There can be no return to previous modes of living, no retreat to the traditional as a way of shoring up identity, or denying rationality and the benefits of science. Such retrogression only lands us in kitsch. But there might be ways into previous kinds of thinking. Pilgrimages, let's say, to newly imagined territories where, instead of arrogantly dismissing the traditional as useless to modernity, the best of each might be integrated.

When Adam Smith talked about the "wealth of nations", he wasn't referring simply to money, but to a whole ensemble of requirements to wellbeing. Perhaps, who knows, the materialist progress we have made since urbanisation, and the values existing before it, could meld into some marvellous, unprecedented syncretism. But if that is too much to expect, at least attention to nomadic modes of thinking might get us closer to finding whatever solutions to the disintegrations of modern life are actually available to us.

So what are the qualities that nomadic cultures tend to encourage? It seems to me that they are the humanistic virtues. The world is approached as a series of complex interactions, rather than simple oppositions, connecting pathways rather than obstructive walls. Nomads are comfortable with uncertainty and contradiction. They are cosmopolitan in outlook, because they have to deal with difference, negotiate difference. They do not focus on long-term goals so much as continually accommodate themselves to change. They are less concerned with the accumulation of wealth and more concerned with the accumulation of knowledge. The territorial personality – opinionated and hard-edged – is not revered. Tolerance, which accommodates itself to things human and changeable, is. Theirs are Aristotelian values of "practical wisdom" and balance. Adaptability, flexibility, mental agility, the ability to cope with flux. These traits shy away from absolutes, and strive for an equilibrium that blurs rigid boundaries.

There are people whose faith in technology is strong enough for them to believe that there are no limitations on us as a species. We will colonise other planets, or find new sources of energy. Our big brains will save us. Others take the gloomy view that we are hardwired for disaster, that wherever we've been, we've destroyed our environment, and we will always do so. Coded into this view is the tacit belief that our fate is determined by our genes, and our brains, far from saving us, are the very organs that have become an evolutionary disadvantage, because we are using them to destroy the resources on which we live – that is, the planet.

It is an irony of our times that while classical nomadism is ending, hypermobility has become the very hallmark of modernity. It is creating the largest shifts of population the world has ever witnessed. Tribes of labourers on the margins of world capitalism, refugees fleeing wars and ethnic cleansing, rural economic and ecological refugees, draining into cities – all these constitute a wandering nation of a hundred million desperate people. Migration is the quintessential experience of our time, and has become the most contentious issue of contemporary politics.

At one end of the spectrum, those hundred million victims of history; at the opposite end, wealthy people enjoying an almost unrestricted freedom of movement. Business executives commuting intercontinentally between home and work; tourists supporting whole economies in underdeveloped countries or buying apartments on vast cruise ships that never dock. And increasingly, there are people like me, who live in several countries, have complex identities and feel allied to more than one culture. We live in what Edward Said called "a generalised condition of homelessness". These new forms of nomadism will shape the culture of the new century in unpredictable ways.

For one thing, they raise questions concerning personal and national identity. The political constructs of homeland, nationhood, patriotism came into being because of a yearning to belong to a spiritual geography. In the nineteenth century, "the nation" seemed a stable, unambiguous entity. But what can such constructs mean in this turbulent, increasingly placeless world where people are forever crossing borders and hybridising?

The paradox is that the new nomadism of the rich is inherently antithetical to the older forms it is replacing. A traditional nomad had an exquisite understanding of her environment. Hers was a peripatetic sense of place, based on the body's rhythm, sensually tuned into the surroundings, and constantly connecting her with others along the pathways. For her there was "no such thing as alone". The modern nomad is not just uprooted from place, but severed from deep connections with other human beings. Local attachments are the same as all other attachments – shallow. Kinship and community bonds become frail and brittle. Not so much a nomad, as a monad.

This is the price paid for a freedom of movement based entirely on whim and wealth. A forgetting of the interconnectedness of all things. "To be rooted is perhaps the most important and least recognised need of the human soul," wrote Simone Weil in 1942. If that is true, then the new nomadism is contributing to modernity's malaise.

Emile Durkheim's study of suicide found that people who had fewer social connections, bonds and obligations were more likely to kill themselves. The more connected we are, the less likely we are to give way to despair. Beyond a basic level of comfort, money makes no difference to that despair.

Detachment from our surroundings is becoming increasingly "normal". We move through the world faster and faster, looking at it, but not being in it. And the more mobile we become, the less sense we have of being sensually enmeshed with our world and interdependent with, responsible for, others. The ultimate version of this placeless, isolated individual is the virtual nomad, plugged into a computer terminal. On the screen, a virtual earth full of trees, birds and butterflies. Outside the window, a wasteland. Staying "in touch" has become purely conceptual.

For us here in Australia, it has been easy to overlook ecological problems, protected as we are by our precarious good luck, but that is changing, and changing faster than predicted. We have managed in just two hundred years to bugger up our country, to cut an ever-widening swathe through its natural resources. The famine, drought and political chaos that we hear of in places like Africa are not temporary aberrations; they are systemic. When the desertification and the salination and the loss of species and the lack of water can no longer be ignored, will such chaos extend out to us, the privileged?

Old Aboriginal people are worried too, by droughts and decreasing bush tucker, but they see this as a natural consequence of being torn away from their ritual duties. There has been such a ripping asunder of their relationships to sacred sites over the years, it is only to be expected that "orphaned" country will be ill and unproductive. Aboriginal people see their role as keeping country and its vitality in trust for all life to come. Other Australians might do well to find ways of sharing that role.

I shall probably be accused of romanticism. (Romanticism: the desire to escape reality rather than apprehend it better.) Or for idealising pre-modern times out of an ignorance of its hardships. But that is not at all my intention. For one thing, I would have died at age twelve without modern medicine. And I should think contemporary Aborigines might baulk at a return to the foraging life, particularly now as the ravages of drought eradicate the last vestiges of the possibility of that method of subsistence. And I would be more than happy to see the benefits of science – good health, less grinding worry, longer life – brought to the Himalayan peasants.

Nor do I think nomads are or ever were greenies in the way we understand that term today. Their cultural practices, like cultural practices everywhere, could become destructive in new settings, and were often slow to change. And Dreamings could be violent and vengeful. Nevertheless cultures based on mobility require the collection, memorising and integration of observations of environmental processes, knowledge systems that over time become encoded into cosmologies.

And one does not have to be a romantic to be in awe of the Dreaming – that marvellous moving and all-encompassing poem to life.

CODA

In every religion I can think of, there exists some variation on the theme of abandoning the settled life and walking one's way to godliness. The Hindu Sadhu, leaving behind family and wealth to live as a beggar; the pilgrims of Compostela walking away their sins; the circumambulators of the Buddhist kora; the Hajj. What could this ritual journeying be but symbolic, idealised versions of the foraging life? By taking to the road we free ourselves of baggage, both physical and psychological. We walk back to our original condition, to our best selves. "House life is crowded and dusty," said the Buddha. "Life gone forth is wide open. It is not easy, living in a household, to lead a Holy Life as utterly perfect and pure as a polished shell. Suppose I shaved off my hair and beard, put on the yellow cloth, and went forth from the house life into homelessness."

SHORT BLACKS

THE AUSTRALIAN DISEASE
ON THE DECLINE of LOVE AND THE RISE OF NON-FREEDOM
RICHARD FLANAGAN

Richard Flanagan's perceptive, hilarious, searing exposé of the conformity that afflicts our public life.

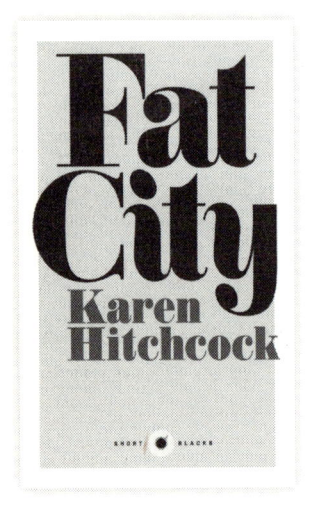

Fat City
Karen Hitchcock

In a riveting blend of story and analysis, doctor and writer Karen Hitchcock explores chemistry, psychology and impulse to excess to explain the West's growing obesity epidemic.

WWW.SHORTBLACKS.COM

CLASSIC SHOTS OF AUSTRALIAN WRITING

THE WAR OF THE WORLDS — NOEL PEARSON

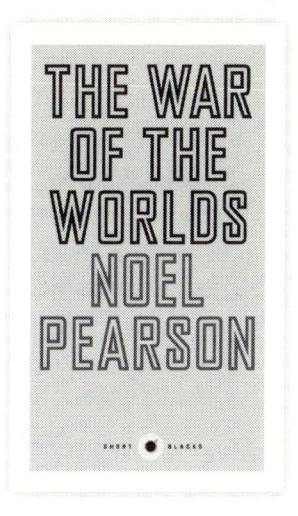

Noel Pearson considers the most confronting issue of Australian history: the question of genocide, in early Tasmania and elsewhere.

REGIONS OF THICK-RIBBED ICE — HELEN GARNER

Helen Garner tells the tale of a journey to Antarctica aboard the *Professor Molchanov*, spanning icebergs, tourism, time, photography and the many forms of desolation.

WWW.SHORTBLACKS.COM

SHORT BLACKS

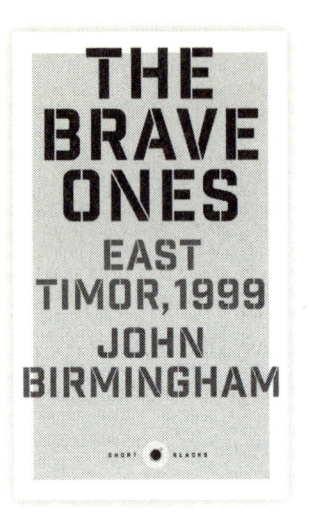

THE BRAVE ONES: EAST TIMOR, 1999
JOHN BIRMINGHAM

John Birmingham's unflinching account of the Indonesian Army's Battalion 745 as it withdrew from East Timor after the 1999 independence vote, leaving a trail of devastation in its wake.

BOOZE TERRITORY
ANNA KRIEN

Anna Krien takes a clear-eyed look at Indigenous binge-drinking, and never fails to see the human dimension of an intractable problem, shining a light on its deep causes.

WWW.SHORTBLACKS.COM

CLASSIC SHOTS OF AUSTRALIAN WRITING

THE ONE DAY
DAVID MALOUF

David Malouf traces the meaning of Anzac Day and shows how what was once history has now passed into legend, and how we have found in Anzac Day 'a truly national occasion.'

Prosper
A voyage at sea
Simon Leys

Simon Leys' exceptionally beautiful and elegiac essay about a summer spent on the crew of a tuna-fishing boat in Brittany.

WWW.SHORTBLACKS.COM

SHORT BLACKS

CYPHERPUNK REVOLUTIONARY
ON JULIAN ASSANGE
ROBERT MANNE

Robert Manne reveals the making of Julian Assange and shows how he became one of the most influential Australians of our time.

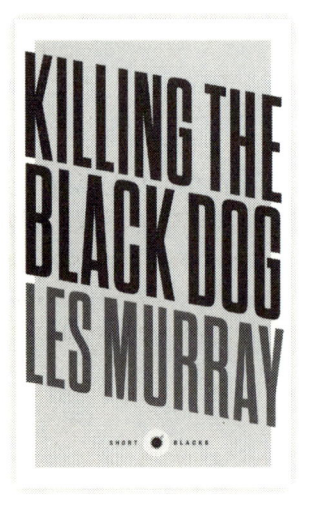

KILLING THE BLACK DOG
LES MURRAY

Les Murray's frank and courageous account of his struggle with depression.

WWW.SHORTBLACKS.COM

CLASSIC SHOTS OF
AUSTRALIAN WRITING

Robyn Davidson's fascinating and moving essay about nomads explores why, in times of environmental peril, the nomadic way with nature still offers valuable lessons.

Galarrwuy Yunupingu tells of his early life, his dealings with prime minsters, and how he learnt that nothing is ever what it seems.

WWW.SHORTBLACKS.COM